[GIVEN, IF, THEN]

[Given, If, Then]

A Reading in Three Parts

Jeremy Fernando

Jennifer Hope Davy

Julia Hölzl

dead letter office

BABEL Working Group

punctum books ∗ brooklyn, ny

[Given, If, Then]: A Reading in Three Parts
© Jeremy Fernando, Jennifer Hope Davy, Julia Hölzl, 2014.

http://creativecommons.org/licenses/by-nc-nd/3.0/

This work is Open Access, which means that you are free to copy, distribute, display, and perform the work as long as you clearly attribute the work to the authors, that you do not use this work for commercial gain in any form whatsoever, and that you in no way alter, transform, or build upon the work outside of its normal use in academic scholarship without express permission of the author and the publisher of this volume. For any reuse or distribution, you must make clear to others the license terms of this work.

First published in 2014 by
dead letter office, BABEL Working Group
an imprint of punctum books
Brooklyn, New York
http://punctumbooks.com

The **BABEL Working Group** is a collective and desiring-assemblage of scholar-gypsies with no leaders or followers, no top and no bottom, and only a middle. BABEL roams and stalks the ruins of the post-historical university as a multiplicity, a pack, looking for other roaming packs with which to cohabit and build temporary shelters for intellectual vagabonds. We also take in strays.

ISBN-13: 978-0692298374
ISBN-10: 0692298371

Cover Images by Jennifer Hope Davy.

for you

Contents

PROLOGUE	i
BLIND READING JEREMY FERNANDO	3
PICTURES JENNIFER HOPE DAVY	21
III JULIA HÖLZL	73
BIOGRAPHIES	99
IMAGE CREDITS	101

PROLOGUE

[Given, If, Then] attempts to conceive a possibility of reading, through a set of readings: *reading* being understood as the relation to an Other that occurs prior to any semantic or formal identification, and, therefore, prior to any attempt at assimilating, or appropriating, what is being read to the one who reads. As such, it is an encounter with an indeterminable Other, an Other who is other than other—an unconditional relation, and thus a relation to no fixed object of relation.

The first reading by Jeremy Fernando unfolds through an attempt to speak of reading as an event. Untheorisable in itself, it is a positing of reading as reading, through reading, where texts are read as a test site for reading itself. As such, it is a meditation on the finitude and exteriority in literature, philosophy, and knowledge; where blindness is both the condition and limit of reading itself. Folded into, or in between, this (re)reading are a selection of photographs from Jennifer Hope Davy's image archive. They are on the one hand simply a selection of 'impartial pictures' taken, and on the other hand that which allow for something singular and, therefore, always other to dis/appear—crossing that borderless realm between 'some' and 'some-thing.' Eventually, there is a writing on images on writings by Julia Hölzl. A responding to the impossible response, a re-iteration, a re-reading of what could not have been written, a re-writing of what could not have been read; these poems, if one were to name them such, name them as such, answer (to) the impossibility of answering: *answer to no call*.

Blind Reading

Jeremy Fernando

Blind Reading

(

Jeremy Fernando

Perhaps we should try to begin by attempting to think what reading is, what it might be—the possibilities of what it can be. And if we are trying to conceive of reading as a response—to the text, to an author, maybe even to reading itself—we have to concede the possibility of never being able to get beyond an attempt. At best, we might be able to gesture at what reading might be.

This is a thinking of reading as a relation to an other that occurs prior to any semantic or formal identification; and therefore prior to any attempt at assimilating what is being read to the one who reads. Hence, reading can no longer be understood in the classical tradition of hermeneutics—as a deciphering according to an established set of rules—as this would only give a minimum of correspondence, or relation, between the reader and what is read. In fact, reading can no longer be understood as an act, since an act by necessity would impose the rules of the reader upon the structure of what (s)he encounters; in other words, the reader would impose herself upon the text. Since it is neither an act nor a rule-governed operation, reading needs to be thought as *an event of an encounter with an other*; an other which is not the other as identified by the reader, but heterogeneous in relation to any identifying determination. Being an encounter with an undeterminable other—an other who is other than other—reading is an unconditional relation, a relation therefore to no fixed object of relation. Thus, reading could possibly be conceived as the ethical relation *par excellence*.

Here, it might be helpful to keep in mind that reading is the starting point of all evil (Paul de Man). And, if we listen carefully, it is not difficult to hear an echo of the serpent, in particular the eternal question of "did God really ask you not to eat from any of the trees in the garden?" (*Gen* 3:1). One must never forget that this is the question that is never answered, for we never actually hear what Yahweh says to the woman; all we can know, ever know, is from her, through her. Moreover, it is not as if the serpent was lying; after eating of the fruit from the tree of knowledge, man and woman do not die—as Yahweh claims—but were instead expelled from the garden as they had gained the knowledge of the gods, just as the serpent said they would. As we never actually hear Yahweh's words, Her command—and only know of the imperative through the woman—we can never constitute the question within the realm of truth and falsity. Without referentiality, we are left with either the notion of the question as performative, or perhaps more radically, as a question that remains a primordial question, the first hermeneutical moment. The question of: *did God really mean what (S)he said?* And since we have no way of knowing—there is no way of legitimately distinguishing the two—we are left with a pure choice; and have to decide on the status of Yahweh's statement without any possibility of knowing whether our choice is right, or wrong.

Thus, a baseless decision, a groundless choice.

But just because a choice is bereft of *grund* does not make it any less of a choice, does not mean there are no effects to that choice, does not mean that others are not affected by it. Since the one who is choosing is making that decision without any basis—at least in the sense of a rational, solid, reason to back one up, fall back on—this opens the consideration that one is also authoring that decision in the moment of making it. However, problems arise when one attempts to link authorship to authority: as if the one who writes, the one who pens down something—in a, in any, situation—writes from above, is master of the scene, scenario, governs, controls it, has a certain divine power over it. But, as Avital Ronell continually reminds us, authority rest upon a figure— and even if it might reach us through the father, an origin (*auctor*), daddy always remains a name for what is unreachable; beyond, one might well say above, one. A figure that remains unquestionable, outside of ratio, reason, quite possibly even knowability. Thus, his authority remains out of bounds: so even as one stands before him, before the law as it were, one is never privy to the source of his authority—whether daddy knows from whence it comes is altogether another question. Which opens the question: *can an author ever know where the authority to call herself an author comes from? Does, can, one even call oneself an author?* After all, not every piece of writing is considered authored: scribblings on a napkin, graffiti on a wall, notes on scraps of paper, etc., are, at best, preludes to an authored text. That is, unless they belong to someone who is established (allowing all echoes of institutions, canons, to resound here): then suddenly everything that they have ever written is deemed part of their *oeuvre*—often times against their expressed wishes. One only has to look at the case of Franz Kafka and Max Brod to see this. This suggests that one's status as an author is granted to one, from elsewhere, from beyond. For, even as it is tempting to place the onus of the status of authorship on publishers, on whether a writer is published or not, this only partially addresses the issue: not every published writer is considered an author. It would still seem that until daddy tells you that you are so, you don't get membership status; and even if that ever happens, it is not like you ever quite, can, know *who's your daddy*.

[Which opens the question of citation. Of, *why we cite as we write*. Of, *seeking authority from another whilst attempting to make one's case for something*. Even if that something is reading; even if one is attempting to conceive of—think—reading as something other than a thing. But even as we cite, we have to remember Paul de Man's warning that "it is impossible to say where quotation ends and 'truth' begins, if by truth we understand the possibility of referential verification. The very statement by which we assert that the narrative is rooted in reality can be an unreliable quotation; the very document, the manuscript, produced in evidence may point back not to an actual event, but to an endless chain of quotations reaching as far back as the ultimate transcendental signified God, none of which can lay claim to referential authority." Whilst this may be so, perhaps de Man might have missed a point: the divine has absolute authority precisely because it has no referentiality. For, with the possibility of correspondence, something can be shown to be true or, conversely, false; without it, one is beyond truth or falsity. And here, one should not forget that even as we name the ones we are citing—even as convention usually dictates that we name the place from where these citations are drawn—citations are always out of context.

Thus, one always draws from the names—rubs shoulders with these figures of authority; which might be why we explicitly designate a space for them through, within, quotation marks—whilst always already rewriting them, making them our own, drawing energy and life from them (which might be why we put vampire marks around them). And even as one draws authority from them, we are always also authorising these citations ourselves: signing off on them, for them; regardless of their wills. Through language; even as language itself is always already a citation, a voice of another; even though "we have been in citation ever since we said the first words mama or papa" (Hélène Cixous). Making what is not ours, ours.

Authoring authority for oneself.

Perhaps hoping that daddy will not notice.]

And even as one may have attempted to author one's own authority, whether it is recognised or not remains unknown to one. Even at the point at which it is accepted, the reason why it is acknowledged remains unknown, remains perhaps tautological: it is accepted because it is. For, the moment one has to prove one's authority, it is gone; one only has authority when one doesn't have to use it. One is only an author when one doesn't have to prove one is so; when one does not even have to name oneself as such. Authority as such lies in its absence.

It remains a secret.

And what could be more secret in the Garden than the intent of Yahweh's statement.

Here, if we listen carefully to the tale of woman, man, and the serpent, we might notice that evil is not antonymic to good, but also its "inner faltering, [its] suicidal crumbling, [its] reversion" (Jean Baudrillard). In other words, evil is the singularity—undefinable, unrepresentable—that resists totality, completeness, unity, certainty. Evil is the enigma that allows us to even ask, *did God really mean what (S)he said,* in the first place. But evil not only prevents a hermeneutic certainty, it is precisely what allows reading to happen in the first place: for, if one could ever know for sure, that would also be the point that reading ceases. It is evil that gives reading its enigmatic status, and maintains the very secret that is reading, that gives reading its life, movement, vitality.

Perhaps here, we should keep in mind that it is a yearning for "metaphysical comfort," certainty, which brings about theorising—as opposed to thinking which is always uncomfortable, discomforting, unsettling—in order to give the *theorist* the false assurance that he knows, that he understands, that he grasps the world in his hands: the ego of the "theoretical man" is satisfied when he can fully explain the world he lives in; where the world is nothing other than his world (Nietzsche).[1] In this manner, there is no longer a joy of living, of living as discovery, with openness

---

[1] Perhaps here, one could open the question of why some citations have—perhaps even require—a full name, or at least a first and last name, whilst a single name suffices for others. Here, one could, quite easily, turn to the notion of celebrity, and posit that a sign of true fame is when no other has access to the name one uses: Elvis, for instance, comes to mind. However, in the case of this chapter, this piece, it is not as if any of the people cited here aren't well known, at least in their own circles. Which opens the possibility that those that require but one name are those who have—somehow, for we do not, perhaps can never, quite know how these things occur, happen—subsumed every other with variations of their name into themselves: almost akin to the case of the monster in *Frankenstein* who seems to have, at least in popular consciousness, swallowed Victor Frankenstein's name. It is rather understandable that quite a number of people think that the monster bears the family name: after all, one could quite plausibly conceive of Victor as his father. What is more

to the possibility of change, flux, chance. Perhaps, only through refusing the notion of complete knowledge can one hope to glimpse life; through the realisation that certainty is an illusionary concept that is a gesture against life itself.

By introducing the question, by attending to Yahweh's statement whilst never allowing it to settle, both the serpent and the woman ensure that Yahweh's command continues to live. After all, what good is a disciplinary mechanism if the subject is completely willing to be subjected: in fact, discipline is not only premised on resistance, it is rendered completely redundant without it.

And, what good is a text if there is no reading?

Perhaps here, it might be helpful to turn to a particular punctuation mark often considered an aberration to writing … the ellipsis. Ellipses mark the fact that there is something more, an addition, or something less, a retraction—not that the two are mutually exclusive, for one could always add in order to retract—in that sentence. It is the mark of an absence in the sentence, but one that affects the sentence; it is an absence that remains to haunt the sentence. However, the manner in which it affects the sentence remains unknown … it is the secret of that sentence. Considering the fact that all knowledge is based on a correspondence between what is said, seen, read, and something that is in the world, this suggests that it is premised on memory: after all, one can only make a relation, conceive of relationality, the second time something occurs. The event, the first time, is always already beyond—perhaps before—the possibility of one's knowing, one's knowledge. And, if we consider the fact that forgetting can occur at any time, in any place, there is no reason to believe that each act of remembering might not bring with it, within in, forgetting. Thus, each sentence brings with it the possibility of an ellipsis; whether we see it or not, is perhaps irrelevant.

This might be a good time to open our registers to the notion, or at least the possibility, that "ellipsis is the rhetorical equivalent of writing: it depletes, or de-completes, the whole so as to make conceptual totalities possible. And yet every conceivable whole achieved on the basis of ellipsis is stamped with the mark of the original loss. Like writing, it withdraws from the alternatives of presence and absence, whole and part, proper and foreign, because only on its ever eroding foundation can conceptual oppositions develop: it withdraws from its own concept. Ellipsis eclipses (itself). It is the 'figure' of figuration: the area no figure contains" (Werner Hamacher). Here, we should also try not to forget that it is forgetting that allows one to write in the first place. For, if everything has already been written—if nothing has been left out, omitted, added to, remixed—there is then, also, nothing left to write. And perhaps, it is only because one can never be sure if one has forgotten that leaves us the space to continue thinking, negotiating, writing. Thus, it is not just that the ellipsis is the mark of forgetting, it is also "the area no figure contains"—and precisely because it is the mark of the non-mark, it is forgetting itself. So, even as it marks, even as there is a mark, it is a mark which "eclipses (itself)"—keeping in mind that it is an "(itself)" that can only be in parenthesis; hidden away within, through, another mark.

---

curious is that quite a number of people draw a blank when asked what the inventor's name was: almost as if the monster had not only taken on his last name, but had stripped him of his name, any name. Perhaps we might even ponder the possibility that the ones who use only one name have rendered all others with their names, or even variants of their names, nameless.

Or perhaps—without meaning to be glib—one could posit that it is a matter of cadence, of sound, rhythm. For, I choose—and this might well only be me—between full and single names based solely on which one sounds prettier.

And, it is this inability to know if we know, to be sure that we have understood, that allows us to continue reading, attending to; that opens the possibility that we have possibly never quite read the text. In other words, each attempt at reading is haunted by the possibility of an event. What remains unknown though is not only whether the event is present, but also its source—whether it occurs in the text, in the reader, in the reading, in the relationality between the reader and her reading, remains secret from us.

But, just because there is a spectre of unknowability does not absolve one from responsibility. For, each reading comes with its moment of violence; each reading is a response to a particularity of the text, to a particular reading, whilst always already being blind to other readings, other possibilities, within that same text. Each reading is a possible reading, a contingent reading, and also a true reading, as truth itself is contingent—on that reading itself. Hence, each reading is a position, a positing, hypothesis; a test site for both what is read and reading itself. Where not only is the reader reading the text into existence (by responding to and with the singularity of the text), the reader is reading herself into existence. For, there is no reader without the reading—no reader outside of reading. Reading is thus, not only the re-writing of the text but also the reading of the reader. Where each reading, each negotiation between the reader and the text, is potentially an encounter; one in which both the reader and the text (and quite possibly the reader and her self) remain completely other to each other.

However, just because reading is potentially an event does not mean that it is a free-for-all, that anything goes. For, to read, one must be "skilled at looking": one must have a certain level of craft; and also know the laws of looking, the laws of reading, grammar itself. And, even as the reader, every reader, has a "right to see," it takes a certain "skill to see," in that it is not a random, purely arbitrary act; (s)he is always already bound by a "law of seeing" (Jacques Derrida). One is free within a certain set of rules, and one's reading is an interjection, an interplay between the reader and the text within the rules laid out, the rules before which both the reader and the text must stand. In order to play the game—of seeing, of reading—one has no choice but observe the rules; even as one may attempt to transgress them, read them. For, one's access to the game, to reading, can only begin with, through, the rules—without a boundary, limits, everything is permissible and thus, not only is nothing permitted, not only is everything rendered meaningless, nothing at all can be said, known, done. For, all acts require a premise—only after which one can determine whether it is good, or bad, or what the significance or signification of the act was—a premise being nothing other than an assumption, an axiom, a threshold, a border. Which does not mean that this premise remains static, stable: for, once the act takes place, there is no guarantee that it does not call its very limits into question, does not stretch the threshold, perhaps even to, beyond, breaking point, does not bring the entire house down, as it were. Thus, reading occurs through the law, grammar, and is also always already potentially the undoing—the reading—of grammar, the law, itself. For, if reading is the negotiation of radical otherness—between the reader and the text—it is an act of creativity, imagination, creation—where a momentary third is formed between, by, the two. And if it is an act of imagination—as opposed to fancy, which is a complete creation in one's mind—it is a negotiation, a thinking of, reading with, reality, with the world around us (Wallace Stevens). How one might fully distinguish a relationality with the world, and a creation solely of one's mind could be called into question: but perhaps the difference lies in the kind of relationship—whilst fancy is solipsistic, imagination is a relationality, a being-with. And since it is a relation with another, this suggests that it is always also already bound by mores, laws, culture itself. Thus, if one is attempting to be imaginative, one has to negotiate these very limits: going directly against the law merely provokes its backlash; taking the law itself to its extremes foregrounds its very limits, perhaps even brings a momentary shudder to its thresholds. The imaginative moment is the reading of the law—is precisely in reading itself. This is why the fragment, the detail, is what is always most subversive: whenever a singularity is examined, explored, thought upon, the totality of a concept falls apart: for, singularity is always an exception, in exception, to the rule. After all, *the devil is in the details.* For, "judgment [like language] engenders the same possibility of reference that it also excises. Its error can therefore not be localized or identified in any way; one could not, for example, say that the error stems from language, as if language were an entity that existed independently of judgment or judgment a faculty that could exercise its activity in a nonlinguistic mode. To the extent that judgment is a structure of relationships capable of error, it is also language. As such, it is bound to consist of the very figural structures that can only be put in question by means of the language that produces them" (de Man). Thus, each reading can, at best, reach the status of a judgment, insofar as a judgment is judging the justness of its judgement as it is judging. Hence, there is the possibility that each reading is the undoing of reading itself—in exception to everything, even the possibility of reading.

And since reading is both bound by, and unravels, its own boundaries, it is a negotiation that does as it cannot do … it is a tautological premise that remains blind to its own possibility, in its own possibilities.

Thus, this is not a blindness that is a refusal to see, an antonym to sight, but rather a blindness that is inevitable, structural. This is not a reading that refuses to respond to the text, but a reading that reads whilst not fully knowing what it reads nor even what reading is. A reading that does not claim to understand, subsume, makes no claims on understanding.

Reading as a continual reading—an unveiling, of the text, the reader, reading itself.

Here, it is not too difficult to hear echoes of Jacques Derrida's meditation on painting; in particular, the moment of blindness inherent in each act of painting. For, at the moment the brush strokes the canvas, the painter has to take her eyes of the object that is being painted: hence, the painting itself is a work of memory. And if instead, the painter keeps her eyes on the object, this means that her stroke, the act of painting itself, will be made in blindness. Thus, in every instance painting is a memorial to blindness—paintings are *memoirs of the blind*. And, if you take into consideration the potential forgetting in every act of memory, every painting is always already a negotiation between remembering and forgetting: a conversation in which "the painting is only the witness who saw what happened" (Yves Klein). This negotiation between memory and forgetting—this moment of imagination—is one that is still bound by the law of seeing, of looking, especially if the painter is attempting to respond with the object of her painting. So, it is not as if the painter is effacing the object whilst painting, but that her act of painting can never have the certitude that the object of her painting is the same object that (s)he is painting.

And, it is this same uncertainty of imagination that reading is fraught with.

And this is what allows us to read, and at the same time never allows us to know if we are writing—bringing with it the problems of authorship and authority—as we are reading.

Thus, reading is a contract between the reader and the text. Keeping in mind that reading is a result of that contract and not a pre-ordained right, not a naturally occurring phenomenon; that the possibility of reading is due to this agreement with the text itself. This suggests that reading can never be extrapolated, universalised, totalised, as referentiality that is both the result and the basis of reading—and language itself—refers ultimately to nothing except itself (de Man). But just because one knows of the existence of the contract does not mean that the terms of that said contract are known, are clear. For, even if one has the "skill to see," one can never verify if what one sees is true—that would require a faith in correspondence, one that is hinged around memory. And if so, this would suggest that a *correct* reading would be a pre-existing reading; a citation, a quotation. If this were so, one then runs the risk of also not reading, of never reading. For, if reading were an event, it cannot also be pre-existing. Unless what is the same is also never quite the same: this would then suggest that reading might lie beyond knowability. In this manner, reading always already escapes verifiability, correspondence, and might well be exterior to cognition.

Perhaps then, all that can be said is that reading is attempted.

Whether there is any reading, or not, can perhaps—at best—be judged in its singularity. Which means—reopening the register that singularity quite possibility undoes, unhinges, conceptual totalities, theories—that a judgment perhaps only can judge as it is judging. Or, even: that any judgment is a singular judgement; one that quite possibly judges itself as it is judging, judges itself as judgment.

Thus, each time there is reading, each time we read something, we have no choice but to imagine the possibility of reading whilst reading; and what is being imagined is reading itself.

At this point, it might be prudent to address a quandary that we are facing. If we insist on the singularity of reading, this suggests that not only will we be unable to determine whether any reading is correct or wrong, we would not even be able to know if any reading has occurred in the first place. Hence, not only are epistemology and hermeneutics called into question, the very phenomenal status of reading is potentially unknowable.

However, to merely say that reading is impossible would not only be insufficient, it would also be plainly false. Even if we do not—cannot—know it, or at least fully comprehend it, it is certainly something that occurs, affects us, has effects on us. This suggests that, at the very least, there must be some form of relationality that occurs whenever we read something. And in order to momentarily examine this, we might slow down and attempt to consider relationality itself through the most basic statement of relation, the very basis of all correspondence—that *something is like something else*.

Each utterance of relation is haunted by the possibility of subjective preference; that this relationality is uttered only because the one who utters it wants it to be so. However, whether it is a biased statement or not might well be moot, even irrelevant; intent can never legitimately be discerned from a statement. What is crucial is the fact that this statement—this relationality— would not be, if it was not called into being by that person. And in order for the person do so, (s)he would first have to assume the possibility of this very relationality; it is only retrospectively that the validity of the statement of relation can be tested. Hence, this is a statement that is based on nothing but the assumption of the possibility of relationality. Thus, the statement of relation is not a statement of reference, of correspondence, but the very naming of referentiality itself.

And since every statement of relation—every relationality—is named, it brings with it all the problems of names: naming the singularity that it is naming; whilst also bringing with it all the historicities, contexts, circumstances of that name, naming everything but that singularity. It is a metaphor insofar as every name is a transference of all the other stories that surround it; at the same time, it resists all transference in its bid to be unique, particular, singular. In this way, every name is a *singular-plurality* (Jean-Luc Nancy). In the indeterminacy between its singularity, and all its potential references, all that can be known is that it is naming. Thus, every name names nothing except the fact that it names; is quite possibly always already in catachresis. And, every reading—every imagining of reading, every imagining that is reading—is precisely the naming of itself as reading.

And, for reading to even occur, one must first assume its possibility. Thus, reading is a pre-relational relationality; and what the reader encounters may only be encountered before any phenomenon. Reading is thus a non-phenomenal event, or even the event of the undoing of all phenomenality.

And, if we are conceiving of *reading* as the name for the possibility of reading, this suggests that it is haunted by a double blindness. For, not only are we blind to other readings each time we choose one, we are always already blind to the very source of reading; the very reason for the possibility of reading remains secret from us, remains potentially also secret from reading. Hence, this is a positing of blindness as that which both allows reading to take place, is the condition of reading, and also its limit.

And, if an unseeable, an unknowable, is not only its finitude, but also—since what is blind in reading is always also potentially non-reading—its exteriority, this suggests that reading is quite possibly objectless. Which reopens the register that, at best, reading is a contract between the reader and her reading, a contract where the terms remain unknown—and is premised on nothing but the assumption of contractuality.

And, it is with the objectlessness of the contract in mind that we reopen the dossier of the secret. For, what is crucial is not so much the content of the secret but the fact that one knows that it is secret, its status as a secret. Even though everyone might know the same fact, it is only when one knows the importance of the fact that makes it vital. For instance, if one uses the name of one's pet as a password, the mere knowledge of that particular sequence of letters in itself is unimportant. It is only when one realises the significance of that name (and thus, the context is everything) that makes it significant. Hence, it is not the content, meaning, the signification, of the secret that is important, but the knowledge of its significance. But, it is not as if the content itself is irrelevant, completely unimportant. For, as we learned from Han-Christian Andersen's *The Emperor's New Clothes*, uttering a secret also unleashes its power, has the potential to destroy everything. For, in testifying to a secret, we are also our testifying to secrets themselves … bearing witness to what we cannot legitimately bear witness to. Perhaps, it was a message that was meant for us alone. Or even: it was a secret that we might not have even known. After all, when the child pointed out that the Emperor was naked, he had no way of knowing that it was even remotely significant. When Abraham raised his knife to murder Isaac, he had no way of knowing that Yahweh would provide a ram for the holocaust; by uttering "my son, God himself will provide the lamb for the burnt offering" (*Gen* 22:8), he had not only spoken the truth whilst lying, more importantly he gave the right answer to the test without even knowing what the test was about, quite possibly without ever knowing that he was being tested. Thus, a secret—even if its contents were known to us, perhaps even if we think that we know its significance—might well continue to be, always remain, secret from us.

However, even if the secret might maintain itself—as secret—from us, might remain beyond us, the fact that we cannot access it also suggests the possibility that we might unveil it, rupture the secret, unwittingly, unknowingly. That when it comes to secrets, *we know not what we do*. Thus, one has to maintain the secret—in this case, hope to maintain the secret of reading as possibility of reading itself—even if one does not quite know what one is maintaining.

Perhaps then, our only hope lies in adopting a paradoxical relationality with secrets. For, it is not as if we can ever choose to forget something the moment we learn of it. Moreover, unlike the child in the tale, we might not have the luxury of foregrounding it. Thus, we are left with the situation of keeping the secret by acting as if we have no idea what the secret is. In other words, we have to remember to forget it; we must maintain a *proper distance* from it. And, in order to maintain a *proper distance*, one must not attempt to bridge the gap between appearances and reality (Jacques Lacan). One has to allow the fantasy of the appearance—that there is a corresponding reality—to play itself out. By attempting to approach too closely, it is not reality itself that collapses—there is no inherent reality, at least not one that we can know—but the very fantasy itself. The moment this happens, everything breaks down. We see this most clearly in instances of phatic communication: politeness—and the fantasy that we genuinely care about the other person, that *how are you* and *how's your day* are genuine questions—is what sustains daily social interaction. Failure to maintain this fantasy, making the mistake of approaching too closely—by mistaking the question as a real question and actually answering it; thus, foregrounding the fact that it was a meaningless quip—results in not only the end of communication, but the very relationships themselves. This is why, "the Church as Institution always perceived zealots as its ultimate enemy: because of their direct identification and belief, they threaten the distance through which the religious institution maintains itself" (Slavoj Žižek). Which is not to say that the quip itself can be ignored: that would also cause a rupture in the relationship; perhaps even a worse one. For, that would be the total effacement of the utterance, and the relationality itself. What has to be done is: one has to acknowledge the utterance by way of another utterance, perhaps even the same one that was directed at one. For, that would be a response that responds *as if* it were responding, as if one were responding to the other: allowing both parties to maintain the fantasy of both communication and—more importantly—the notion that they had, were part of, a relationship.

In terms of reading, failure to maintain a *proper distance* from the text would take the form of an attempt to find the origin, the truth, of the text by way of a correct, or even a real, reading: the result of which is that the possibility of reading would collapse. For, if we foreground the very fact that we cannot read, that we might not ever know what reading is, we run the risk of undoing the very possibility of being affected by the text, thus, never open ourselves to the effects of the text. Hence, the very possibility of reading might well be closed *a priori*. And, even though the relationality that is required in order to read might always already be only an assumption, its unverifiability does not discount the possibility that the text changes us in a certain, perhaps ultimately unknowable, way.

And what else is a proper distance—gap—but the space of irony.

Reading *as if* we can read.

Reading *as if* reading itself were possible.

Perhaps here, it might be apt to temporarily reopen the dossier of the law. Keeping in mind that since I am positing—and I should take responsibility for my position, for my reading of reading—that reading involves rules, laws, which affect us in ways which may not be entirely clear, and could well remain hidden from us, this suggests that the reader is always standing before a law, one that holds sway over her, and perhaps even judges her, without being entirely visible to her. A situation that is not all that dissimilar from the one K faces in *The Trial* where he is affected by forces that are beyond his comprehension. This is due to the fact that K is faced with a law that he must approach, and which has power of judgment over him, but at the same time, is a law that is hidden from him. And it is this that the priest attempts to highlight to him through the famous parable of the Law:

> *Before the Law stands a doorkeeper. A man from the country comes to this doorkeeper and requests admittance to the Law. But the doorkeeper says that he can't grant him admittance now. The man thinks it over and then asks if he'll be allowed to enter later. 'It's possible,' says the doorkeeper, 'but not now'* …. (Kafka)

It is not that the man is not allowed into the Law, just not at this very moment. And as there is no time stipulation to "but not now," it is not that the doorkeeper is lying to him but that the moment of admittance is deferred. But, just because the Law remains veiled does not mean that it has no effects: we should not forget that the man from the country waits outside the doorway till the end of his life, and in the larger context of the novel, K's trial fully occupies his daily existence, destroys his life, and most probably directly results in his death. Both of them are completely consumed by the Law, even as they remain blind to it. The unknowability of the Law becomes even more curious if we take into account the fact that the doorkeeper tells the man: "no one else could gain admittance here, because this entrance was meant solely for you." Which opens the register of the paradox that every law—that the Law itself—faces. For, in order for something to be Law it has to have a certain universality, in that it is applicable to everyone without distinction or discrimination; however, each application of the Law is singular, unique, situational. At best, the Law can only be known, glimpsed, at the very moment in which it is applied—to the man, to K, to you—but can never be known as such. And, this is why the priest tells K: "you don't have to consider everything as true, you just have to consider it as necessary." For, it is not so much that one cannot differentiate between what is true and what is not, but, more radically, that each truth—and each lie—is only provisional, situational, singular. It is the situationality of the Law that the "commentators" allude to when they say: "the correct understanding of a matter and misunderstanding the matter are not mutually exclusive." And here, one might even posit that within every understanding lies a misunderstanding. But, just because understanding and misunderstanding may be indiscernible does not remove the reader's—my—responsibility. After all, like Kafka teaches us, it is not as if we are compelled to stand before the law. At no point is the man forced to remain. In fact, it is the doorkeeper that is duty-bound to stand there, at least until the man chooses to leave. If anything, it is the text that is compelled to remain before us, as long as we choose to attend to it, attempt to read it.

But since I have posited that one has to adopt an ironic distance towards reading, one can, at best, only assume that one is reading. Thus, one can strictly speaking never know if one has read—one can also never be sure if one's reading has happened before. In this way, the spectre that haunts every work of reading, every attempt at reading, is that of the origin (*auctor*); of whether what one is attempting to do has already been attempted, or even worse, accomplished. After all, no one wants to be deemed a mere reproducer. Here, one can see a trace of an obsession with beginnings, and the fantasy of the original; along with a longing for the aura that surrounds the first, the beginning, and the power it brings with it—the power of credibility, authority, of being the source. The underlying logic is that in order for anything to be important, one has to be the first to do it; more importantly, traces of all others have to be wiped away. In other words, one has to produce, and not reproduce.

Perhaps here, it might be helpful to turn to a strange source, in particular when it comes to reading: Andy Warhol. For, he showed us that it is not so much the reproduction itself that is art, but the very gesture of recognising the objects to be reproduced: the art lies in recognising the possibility of art in the objects through their reproduction. This is not to say that his craft is not craft at its highest level. However, what elevates his craft into art is the ability to trans-substantiate—and here we should remember Plato's teaching that art only comes from, through, the divine—the reproduction into something more than what is reproduced. In this sense, one can posit that Warhol was an author in that moment of recognition; creating a singularity by arresting a particular moment in time. And since it is a singular moment, it is in some sense always also an original gesture; one that has never happened before, one that is also potentially non-repeatable. In the same way, one can posit that every singular response, every reading—like every artistic gesture—is a reification of time: the concretisation of a moment, as if that moment was real; the authoring of a moment.

The irony, of course, lies in the fact that every reading is always already a reproduced gesture, an act of memory. This is not to say reading is solely a recollection. Far from it. For, if we are attempting to approach reading as a response to the text, this suggests that every reading is also potentially a different one. However, the only way in which that could happen is if there were always already the possibility of forgetting, not just in every previous reading, but in that very reading that one is undertaking. Hence, the possibility of a singular reading is premised on the very impossibility of knowing not only if one has read, but if one is even reading; premised on unreadability itself.

But, since it is impossible to know, let alone foreground, what one cannot know, this suggests that reading is in its *praxis*, and more than that, it is always already only to come. This is an approach to reading that acknowledges that part of reading always lies outside the person; that might only be glimpsed momentarily. This is reading as an art in the precise sense of a craft at its highest level, where it consumes the practitioner, often in ways which are exterior to one's cognitive ability: it remains invisible to one; at best, it expresses itself through one.

And if one can never be sure of the status of one's reading—whether it is reproduced through memory, or whether it is a new reading due to a forgetting—every reading is then both (n)either a first (n)or a reproduction. Thus, all that can be said is that reading is a gesture towards the possibility of reading.

Where reading itself might always remain a secret from us. And more than that, since reading always already remains potentially exterior to the person, there are no readers; there is only the possibility of the gesture.

One that is made in blindness to everything but—perhaps even to—the possibility of reading ….

Yanyun Chen, *Oktopod*, 2014

An Afterword—or, In the Beginning there was …

An Afterword—Or, In the Beginning There Was …

Plato teaches us that learning occurs through mimesis. Thus, all knowledge is a form of repetition. However, its highest point, zenith—wisdom—only comes to one; at the point where one opens oneself to the possibility of the whispers of the *daemon*. This is not to say that wisdom is antithetical to knowledge, learning, mimesis—but that it is at its very limits, and perhaps is even exterior to it. So, even as all earnest learners strive to be wise, wisdom is the point where the one who remembers, learns, no longer remembers that (s)he is remembering; the point in which one is moved by wisdom itself. Where mimesis is no longer just mimetic; where repetition is never quite the same.

This is perhaps why plagiarism has long been the boogey-man of academia. Not because of any moral grounding (if all knowledge is based on a form of repetition, all writing is always already an echo, plagiarised) but, more pertinently, that there is no way to differentiate between what is written—momentarily leaving aside differences between writing and authorship—and what been taken, stolen, remixed. And here, one should not forget Friedrich Nietzsche's teaching that writing (*schreiben*) is haunted by a scream (*schreien*), a cry. And here, as we hear the cry, we might attend to the possibility that it is a scream of frustration due to the inability to separate the one who creates and the one who records: a dual note that can quite possibly be heard in the figure of the scribe. [And here, we might even open the dossier, the possibility, that, perhaps the inscriber and the one who transcribes are always in a duel—keeping in mind, or at least trying not to forget, that duels are only possible, are premised on, there being duality, at least a duo.]

However, it would be too quick, too fatalistic, to stop here. For, as both Nietzsche and Gilles Deleuze constantly remind us, repetition is not necessarily the same. This is best captured in the colloquial saying one often hears in Thailand: *same same but different*. One can be cynical and claim that it is a mere sales pitch, an attempt to charge more for the same thing—where it is nothing but a performative claim of difference. After all, one hears this phrase mostly from shopkeepers who have been accused of charging more than another vender for the same item. However, if one does so, one would be missing the possibility of attending to another reading: that one can only make a claim about something in a specific situation; that the same thing in another context is also different—that all claims are singular. Which opens the dossier that an object is never just an object: if one is attempting to attend to it, one has to respond to it in its throwness into the world. Even more pertinently, *same same but different* opens the possibility that difference(s) can lie beyond our cognition, outside of, exterior to, our knowledge; that what we know is bound by our phenomenological finitude. That—as Plato has taught us—to truly know we have to be inspired, struck from elsewhere. But since the divine is transcendental, always already beyond us, there is no way of knowing if we are inspired or not, if we are hearing the whispers of the *daemon* or merely voices in our head; if our repetition is really any *different*, or just *same same*.

And whenever we hear the phrase, we should also not forget that *same* appears twice, as a pair, in tandem, as a duo. Perhaps, we might consider the possibility that the duality, the doubling of the *same* draws our attention to the fact that something can only be different when there is someone else to be different from. Which is not to say that difference itself, difference only, relies on another; however, without an other (even if this other is itself at another moment, situation, context) there cannot be any difference. Thus, even as every statement relies on relationality, this very relationality also foregrounds difference; this relationality also reminds us that *same* is like *same* but is not necessarily the *same*; a duality that continues dueling whilst never ceasing, cutting, enacting a *caesura* on being a duo.

Thus, *same-ness* and *difference* are not necessarily antonyms, but always already rely on each other, are potentially part of each other.

Which brings us back to mimesis and repetition. Not forgetting that each time we write, even if it is a direct quotation, it is always in a different context. So, even the same words, in the same syntax, are already in difference. And if we take into account the notion that all reading is based on *a priori* learning, reading is only possible due to a repetition—a correspondence born of mimesis. The trouble is, writing only comes into being when it is read. Thus, each moment of reading is inseparable from the possibility of a re-writing. A re-writing that might occur as *same same* might well be *different*.

Thus, each attempt to read—to attend to the text—to begin reading, is haunted by the spectre of beginnings that cannot begin: for, if all knowing requires a return of the same—or at least a similarity—then one can never quite have a beginning.

Elliptical hauntings.

Where an ellipsis is, ellipses are, the spectre that resides with, in, within, all sentences, all writing; a haunting that never allows the residence to be completely familiar; that haunts my, our, your haunt.

That opens the possibility of the sameness in difference, the difference in the same.

…

Jeremy Fernando
28 May 2014

Pictures

Jennifer Hope Davy

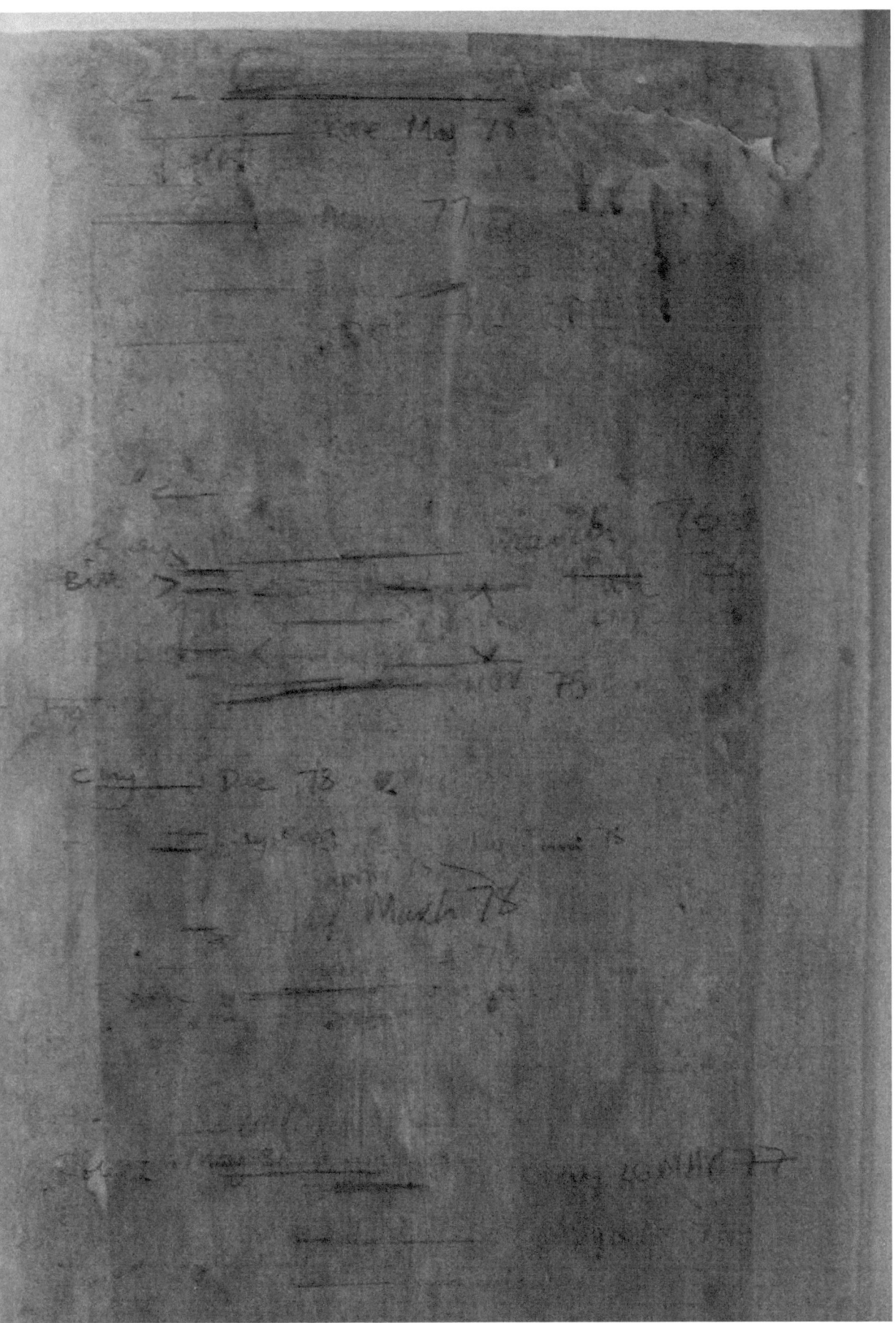

	BOOK NO.	BILL NO.
R.502	274	10

FOOD ORDER

TABLE _____ FL. _____ ROOM _____ PERS. _____ DATE 3/10/11

DESCRIPTION	QTY.	AMOUNT
water	1	20
Fried chicken	1	220
Hot coffee	1	50
	TOTAL	290

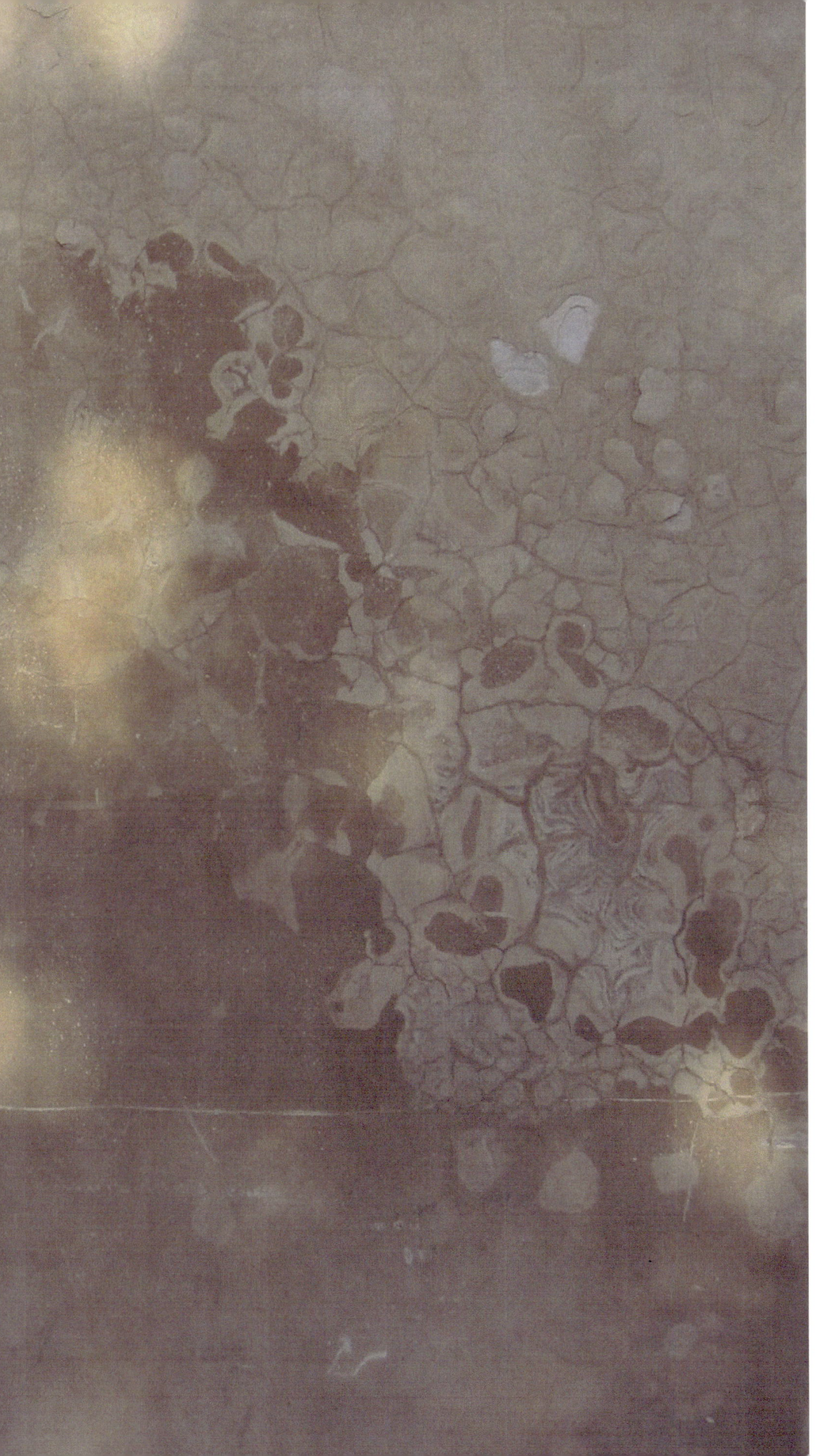

III

Julia Hölzl

1.

and it is thus that I say.
for, says the image,
to say an image
is to say the image as image.

for the image, says the image, says every image, perhaps,
says, of course, nothing but this:
noli mi dicere
and this is, of course, to say
that the image, as celan's poem, does speak
does speak.

2.

what is there to be
if this,
if this there is

no is for this,
for real,
and what is there to be

if such is
this "as is"
if there is

no here in there,
and what if

the here a/s such
and all this
and all this:

because a perhaps does suffice

3.

outside, certainly, but from where
where,to
such outside
obtuse meanings, of course
but what for

oscillating, yes

neither from within, nor to the without; from inside, from outside,
and blah

a reflected perhaps
a double meaning, sure, perhaps even a *neutre*

but why this ambiguity
why this either and, and sides,
when there is nothing
nothing to begin with
why not
just no where,
to begin with

4.

speaking of absence; speaking of which:
which, then

presence presences its absence, we insist

sure, why not,
but why such to and fro,
why always from there

never as such never a such,
when *there is*, no fore no after but

es gibt, perhaps
a moment

enigmatic plainness
descending in,to *nostalgie*
empty slogans, *Leerzeichen*
sissy negation, all affirmation
and nothing but *this*

but this is to read, read this:
that nothing is what there is, and first of all nothing beyond, as reads blanchot

5.

pale questions, as per advice
who am i, she asks, why make me

but who is she
to be said
but who am I to say
to say I,
who says I,
says I

who are you to be you, to begin with
with whom to begin, and where, from
« *je* » *est un autre* etc.
we know
but alas, if only there was less rimbaud and more

6.

where else
no here for this there, we remember
neither absence nor presence, once more
but more:
because seriously,

a lingering
past, present, future, and shangri-las
we remember
day that is no(t) night:
Dämmerung,
"a vague, twilight glow," and this existence, writes blanchot reading kafka, is an
 exile; not there, we are elsewhere,
where else

7.

yes, where
instead a toward, instead the from, the a-byssos, *grund-los, grundlos*,
un-founded, unfounded,

from where, then
and it is from this conciliating vagueness that we should leap

no opening, no closure, ou-topian fragility
no entrance thus
but a dawning, this perhaps

8.

that nothing is what there is, and first of all nothing beyond
that perhaps
nothing is, this first of all

9.

a beginning?
a blanchotian *pallid daylight without depth*

but from where
in the first place
its first place, of course,
from when, then, to think this light,
lacking day, lacking locale

for who dares to think of light as being light

but seriously
wherefrom does light take its lightness
its lack of depth
when all we know are opposites

clarity, citing blanchot, as *the non-light of light, the nonseeing of seeing*

how not to see: such is to think, perhaps

10.

staging
enacting the something to stand
but never on-, and never for its own

a-scriptions of a late presence yet to pass
pre-emptiness

its coming always yet to come, a *vor-wegnahme* of sense
futile in-scriptions

do not de-scribe me, pleads thus the image,
do not tell me

11.

a whole, where
(why remains absurd)

the fragment, fragmenting a/s fragment,
nothing more, no less,
embraces not the lack
does not shatter, nor break
does no/t outside

is elsewhere, where else,

is no/t plural but on(c)e

12.

ainsi toute la philosophie est comme un arbre, writes descartes,
and, asks blanchot, *is there any writer who could not succeed in making a tree talk?*

but how without symmetree
without metes, and bounds, and rhythm,

how to begin

13.

from the side where elsewhere is affirmed

where presence must no longer be
but could [be], whatever

14.

still, a mourning for presence
in heideggerian anticipation we *are:*

my death is mine
certain-ly
yes,
but not-yet, but being-ahead, being-possible, and possibly impossible
etc

yes
but really,
why always just stick to the potential

15.

to abandon: to put halt to presence
as if

for how to leave a/s something

16.

chances are
that, says blanchot, *there is no luck for luck, and that the only luck would be in this anonymous relation that itself could not be called luck, or only this luck that does not fall due*

aporetic opening, to begin with,
but no chance—cadens, cadere, falling— for chance,
auf keinen fall,
but nothing but chance

for how without chance
how out-side the end

17.

that re-presenciation
[of what could not have been present]
(perhaps: a/s perhaps)
is, yes, to affirm:

but to affirm without yes

without the perhaps

but there is an out there

18.

heideggerian being-in-the world: *mitsein,* being-with, *being-with-one-another*

to think! that we could be several

in this

19.

to answer to no call
we must, with heidegger, *we must stay with the question*

20.

there exists, for houellebecq, in the middle of time, the possibility of an island

as if there existed, for me, the possibility of a sea;
of a middle;
as nowhere

21.

and still,
a primal scene?

what happens then: the sky, the same *sky, suddenly open, absolutely black and absolutely empty, revealing (as though the pane had broken) such an absence that all has since always and forevermore been lost therein — so lost that therein is affirmed and dissolved the vertiginous knowledge that nothing is what there is, and first of all nothing beyond.*
, writes blanchot

that perhaps *there is*,
that, perhaps, there *is*

22.

and still, where to begin
when to begin might mean nothing
but this
when where to begin

23.

when there is neither
when all there is is this

what, then, to erase, and where
what, then, to obliterate, and when

being cannot be
duh

24.

remember to restore absence
re-cover its absence:
conceal concealment, perhaps

lethe; etc

25.

ex,ponere, putting forth, originating its origin, to be originated
first, of all
to expose oneself to the feeble gesture
of pointing toward an elsewhere

26.

but, writes blanchot, *when the other is no longer the remote, but the neighbor whose proximity weighs upon me to the point of opening me to the radical passivity of the self, then subjectivity—subjectivity as wounded, blamed, and persecuted exposure, as vulnerability abandoned to difference—falls in its turn outside of being. then it signfies the beyond of being, in the very gift—in the giving of the sign—which its immeasurable sacrifice delivers to the other.*

then—yes, then, and only in such then—
being gifts itself
beyond being

27.

to have done with the judgment of god
but, nietzsche:
man of renunciation, all this you wish to renounce? who will give you the strength for that? nobody yet has had this strength!

all this is what I wish to renounce
for what is to renounce than to affirm
that there is
in such is

28.

feigning indifference
that it is difference which reminds us of sameness
fragile equanimity
that everything is the same,
all the same,
same same but difference,

29.

toward the end, to each and all their ending
and how to end an end

and from where

30.

how can we live without the unknown before us?, asks and cites blanchot rené char,

how can we not

the unknown is to remain
is no(t) potential,
is nothing *to come*
is what eludes,
speaks our desire

not know how to live with—

"Mit allem, was darin Raum hat,
auch ohne
Sprache."
(Paul Celan)

31.

hyped, hyphenated, same same anyway
except the tiring different
of course
there must be what differs
must differ
because

time and again,
and, again, time

and when to think time

32.

to ascribe the image
an image
the eidos as the look, writes heidegger, *anticipated in imagination,*
of what is to be formed gives the thing with regard to what this
thing already was and is before all actualization.

what we need to re-call is this:
that all there is
is the unknown *before* us

33.

to inscribe the image an image —
is to imagine
that there be an outside the image
but,
says blanchot,
the realm of the imaginary is not a strange region situated beyond the world, it is the world itself

this is, and
this is what the world means to me
means this world to me

34.

no beyond, and precisely elsewhere
someone else's
not beyond, and precisely here:
it is not here, and yet it is not anywhere else. nowhere? but then nowhere is here
, writes blanchot

a/s here, no where

* * * *

Contributors

Jennifer Hope Davy is an artist and writer whose work moves between the poetic and the parodic, largely operating in the form of a gesture, an act or a proposition. She was born and raised primarily in Jersey (New Jersey). She has studied, worked and wandered in various countries across the globe and is now currently in situ. Davy received her Fine Arts degree from the San Francisco Art Institute, her Masters in Art History and Criticism from the University of Texas San Antonio and completed her PhD at the European Graduate School (EGS), where she is currently a post-doctoral fellow, focusing on contemporary art as an apparatus of mobility within aporetic junctures. Forthcoming are the books, *Staging Aporetic Potential* and *Pedestrian Stories*. In addition to art and writing, Davy has functioned as a critic, curator, editor, producer and professor of art and media studies.

Jeremy Fernando is the Jean Baudrillard Fellow at the European Graduate School, where he is also a Reader in Contemporary Literature & Thought. He works in the intersections of literature, philosophy, and the media; and has written eight books — including *Reading Blindly*, and *Writing Death*. His work has also been featured in magazines and journals such as *Berfrois*, *CTheory*, *TimeOut*, and *Vice*, amongst others. Exploring other media has led him to film, music, and art; and his work has been exhibited in Seoul, Vienna, Hong Kong, and Singapore. He is the general editor of both *Delere Press* and the thematic magazine *One Imperative*, and a Fellow of Tembusu College at the National University of Singapore.

Julia Hölzl is the Maurice Blanchot Fellow at the European Graduate School, where she also received her PhD. Currently completing a second doctorate at the *Centre for Modern Thought* at Aberdeen University, her present research focuses on the notion of finitude in Blanchot and Heidegger. Julia has studied and taught a variety of disciplines in the humanities and social sciences in Austria, Germany, Spain, Switzerland, the United Kingdom, and Thailand, where she has been a Visiting Professor at the Institute of International Studies at Ramkhamhaeng University (Bangkok) since 2009. Book publications include *Transience. A poiesis, of dis/appearance* (Atropos Press, 2010).

A Note on Image Credits

Jennifer Hope Davy

I am taking this note to acknowledge my former partner, Guy Hundere, and his indelible role in the development of my image archive and, as well, in the actual taking of pictures. Living and working together/separately as artists, lines are bound to be blurred, inspirations interspersed, ideas shared and expressions co-mingled.

More pragmatically speaking, for many years I was without a proper camera and I shared Guy's first generation digital camera. This entailed shooting pictures myself of course, but it also entailed shooting "together" at times: I ask him to shoot something; he asks me to shoot something; we spy our eyes on something to be shot by whomever has camera in hand, and so on. To complicate matters further, we also developed and shared an image archive. Therefore, in this project, which entailed sifting through thousands of images to respond in 34—some images are thus "blind."

Rather than chronicle each more-or-less "blind" image, I've simply notated those with an asterisk. More importantly, regardless of weighted credit, I would simply like to thank Guy Hundere for sharing ways of seeing, and not seeing, together/separately, with me; and to acknowledge the many ways of seeing, and not seeing, we all share by simply being in the world together/separately.

IMAGE CREDITS: JENNIFER HOPE DAVY (*AND/WITH GUY HUNDERE)

1	*Untitled*, 2006 *
2	*Untitled*, 2001 *
3	*Untitled*, 2003
4	*Untitled*, 2003 *
5	*Untitled*, 2003 *
6	*Untitled*, 2009
7	*Untitled*, 2009
8	*Untitled*, 2010
9	*Untitled*, 2001 *
10	*Untitled*, 2010
11	*Untitled*, 2010
12	*Untitled*, 2013
13	*Untitled*, 2013
14	*Untitled*, 2010
15	*Untitled*, 2010
16	*Untitled*, 2011
17	*Untitled*, 2011
18	*Untitled*, 2011
19	*Untitled*, 2011
20	*Untitled*, 2011
21	*Untitled*, 2011
22	*Untitled*, 2012
23	*Untitled*, 2011
24	*Untitled*, 2013
25	*Untitled*, 2013
26	*Untitled*, 2011
27	*Untitled*, 2011
28	*Untitled*, 2012
29	*Untitled*, 2012
30	*Untitled*, 2012
31	*Untitled*, 2013
32	*Untitled*, 2013
33	*Untitled*, 2013
34	*Untitled*, 2006 *

W. dreams, like Phaedrus, of an army of thinker-friends, thinker-lovers. He dreams of a thought-army, a thought-pack, which would storm the philosophical Houses of Parliament. He dreams of Tartars from the philosophical steppes, of thought-barbarians, thought-outsiders. What distance would shine in their eyes!

~Lars Iyer

www.babelworkinggroup.org

www.ingramcontent.com/pod-product-compliance
Lightning Source LLC
Chambersburg PA
CBHW041513220426
43661CB00048B/1545